AF480620

Illustrated FISHING GEAR

Erik Kokkonen

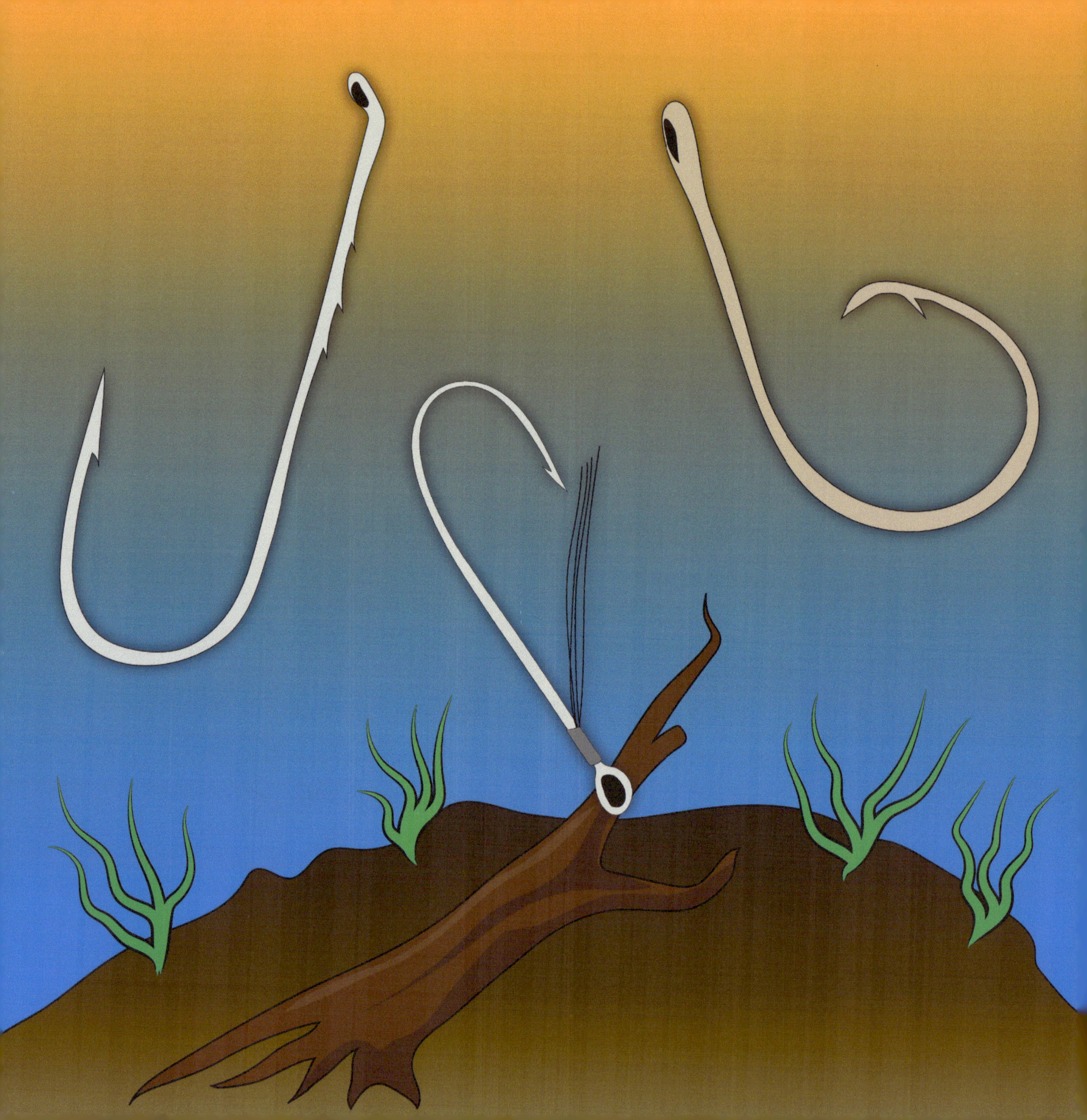

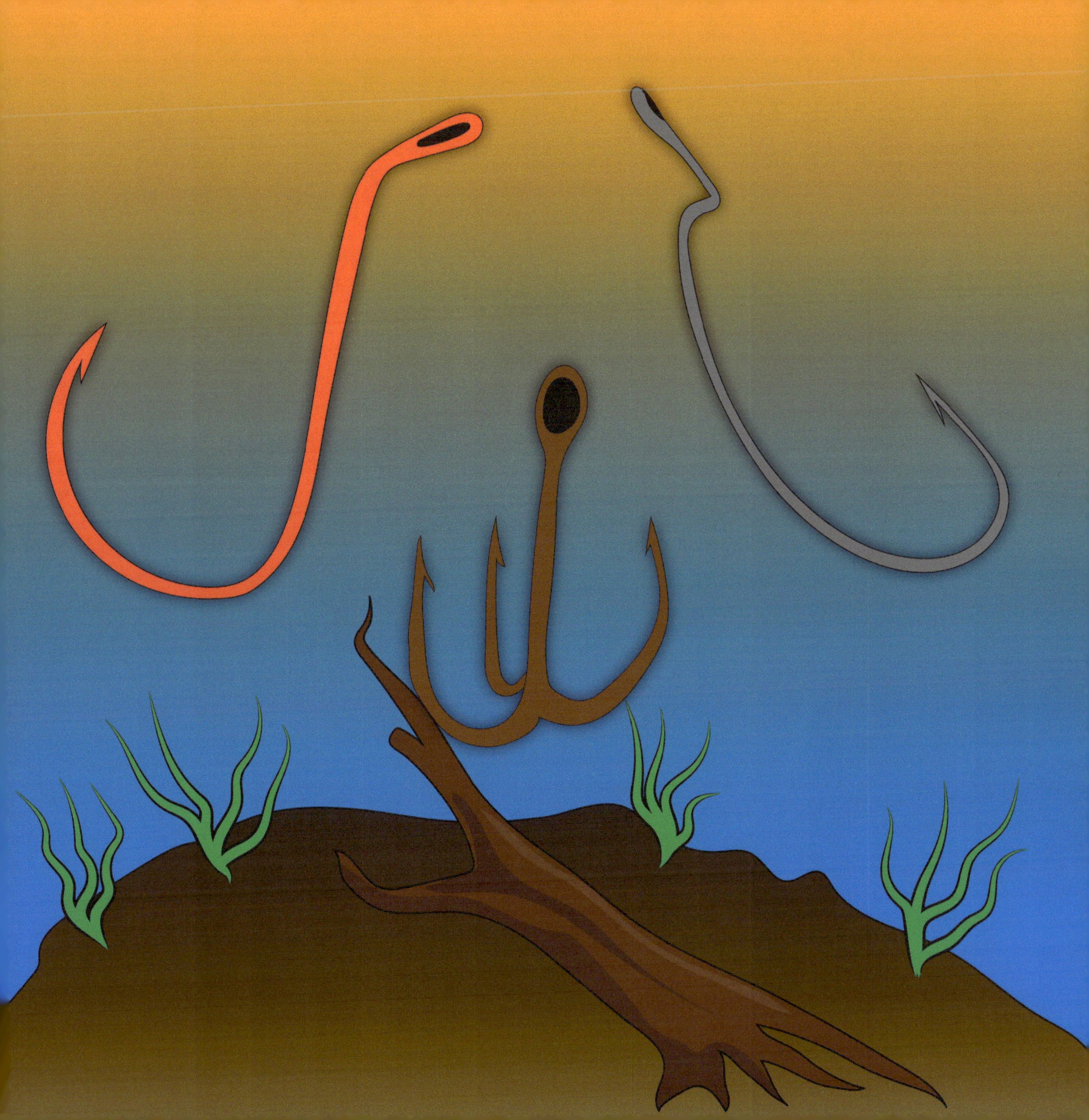

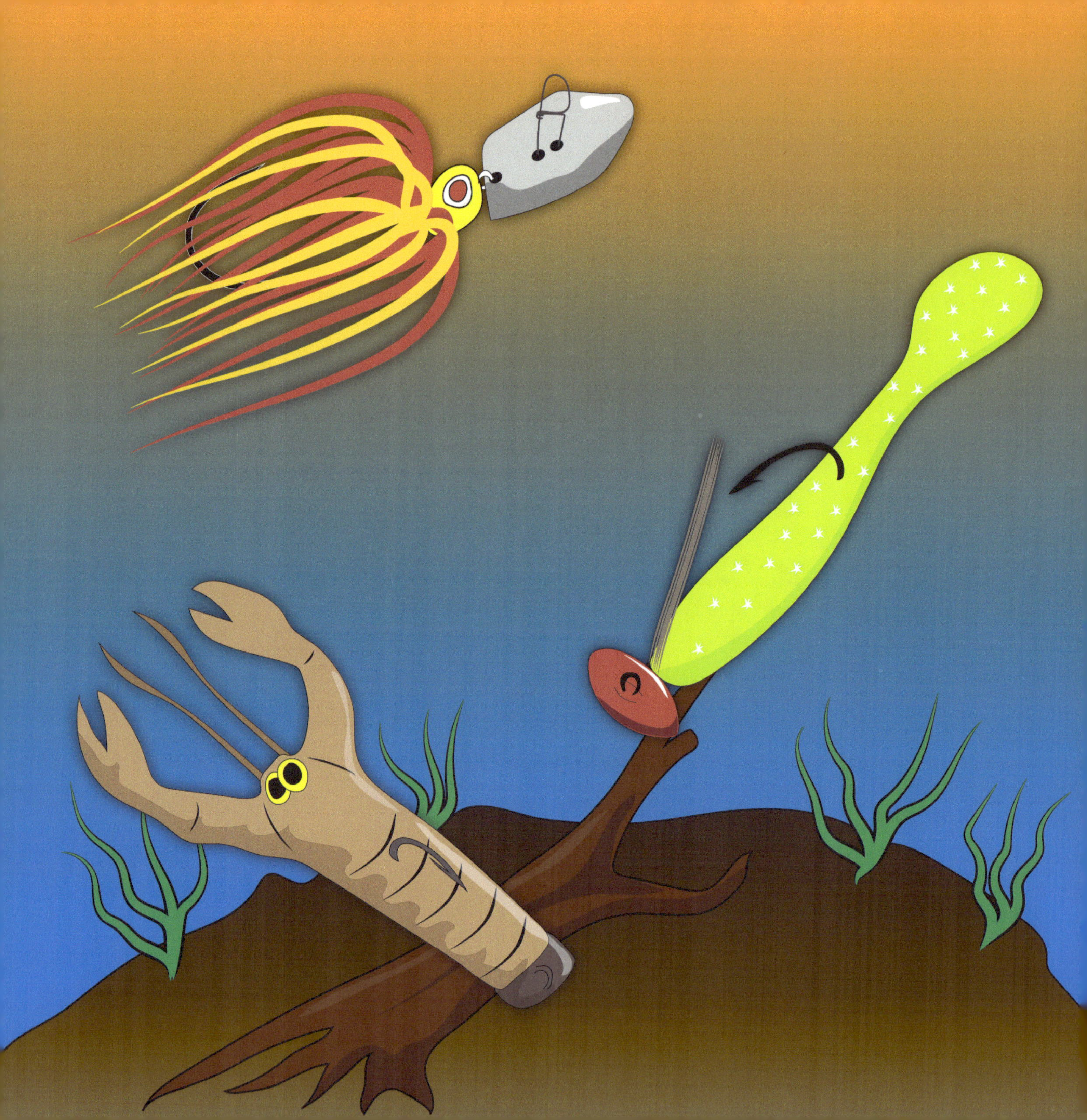

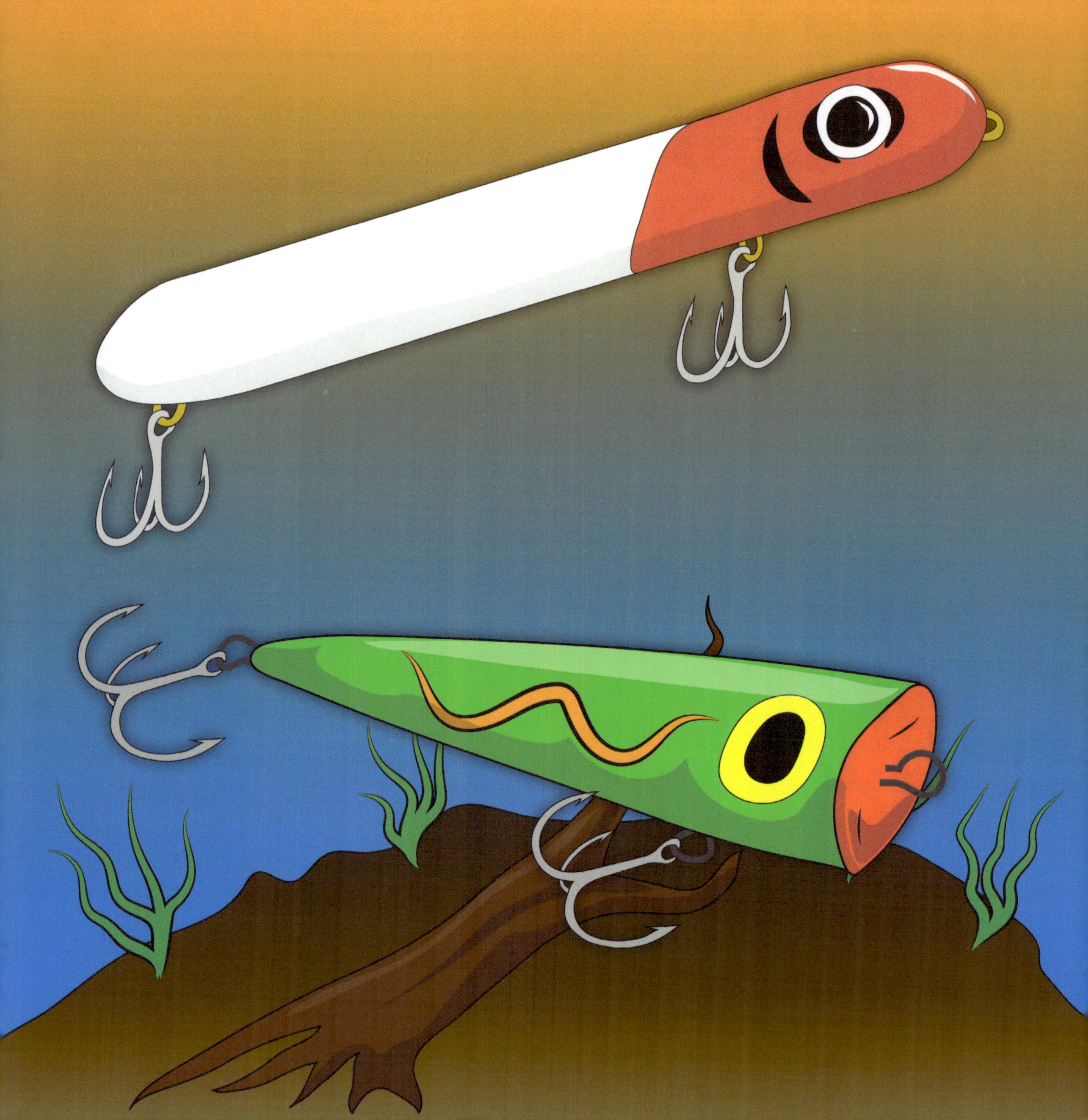

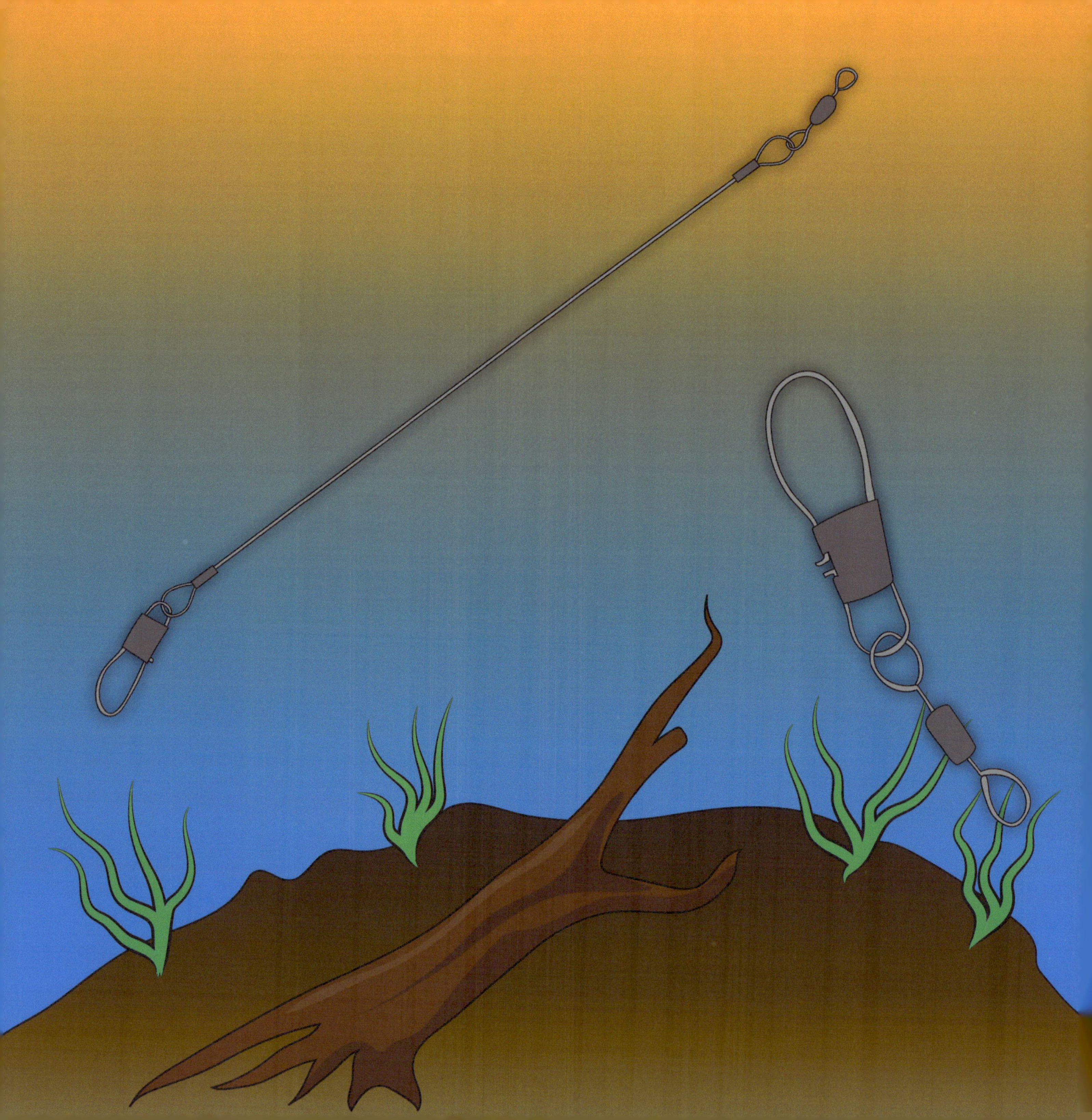

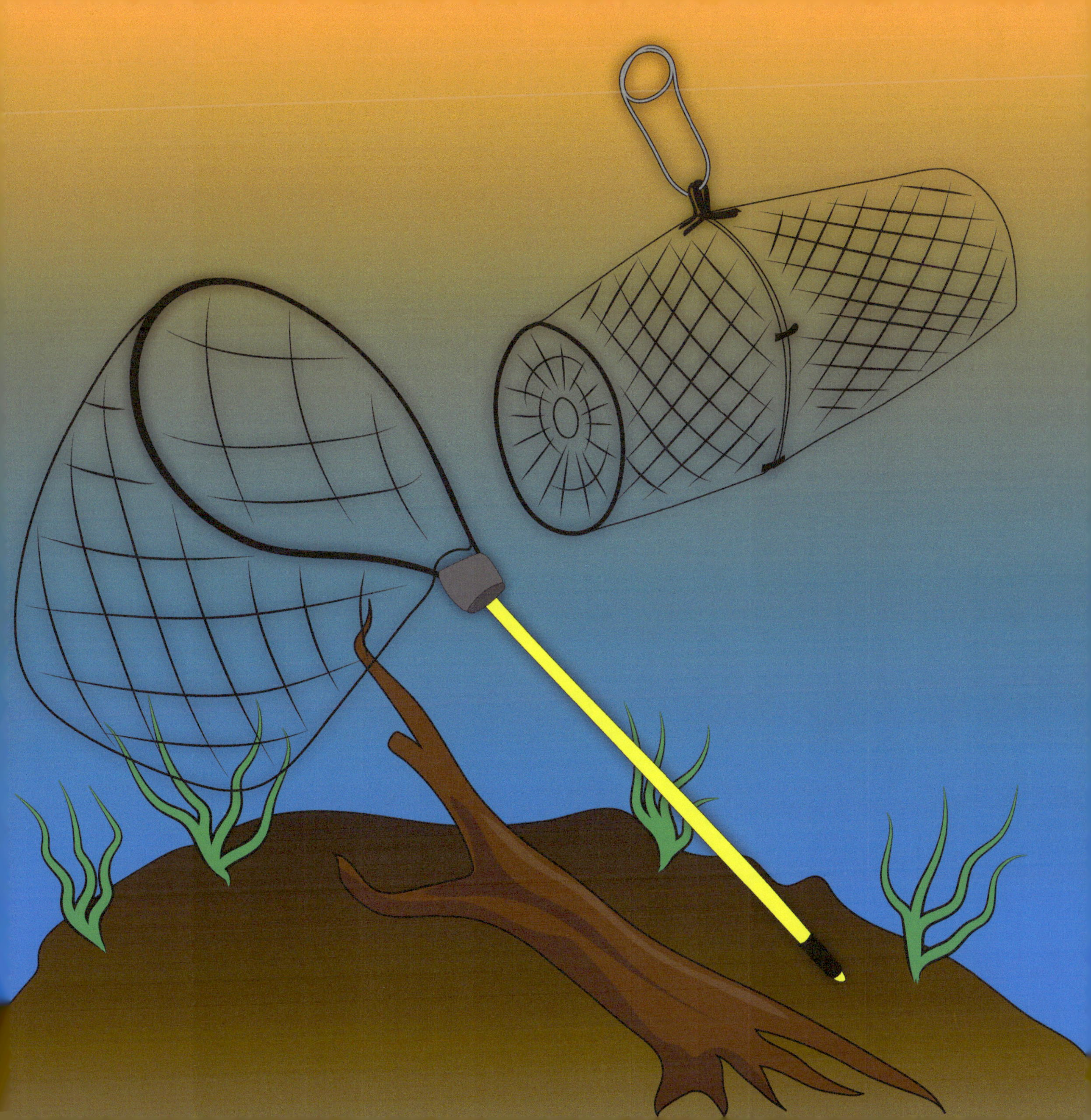

Bait Hook
Circle Hook
Octopus Hook
Swim Bait Hook
Weedless Hook
Treble Hook
Drift Float
Slip Bobber
Fixed Bobber
Classic Red and White Bobber
Coin Sinker
Bullet Sinker
Rubber Core Sinker
Bell Sinker
Split Shot

Wacky Rig
Gumball Jig
Jointed Jerkbait
Tube Jig
Crankbait
Spinner
Blade Bait
Jerkbait
Surface Frog
Popper
Jitter Bug
Spoon

Snagless
Sinker

Chatter Bait

Crawfish Jig

Gumball Jig
With Grub

Swim Bait

Weedless
Football Jig

Spin Bait

Spin Jig

Jigging
Minnow

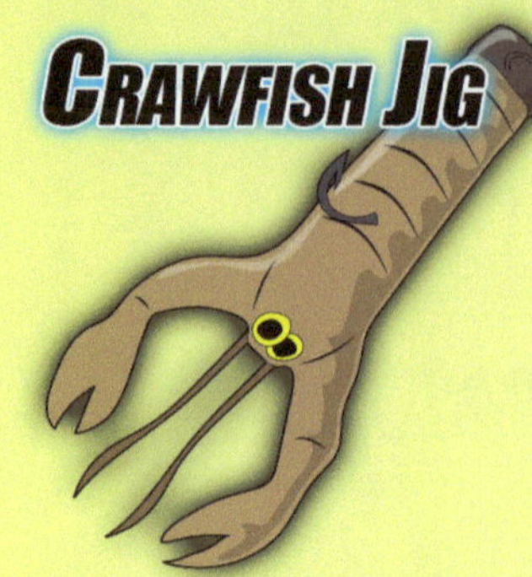

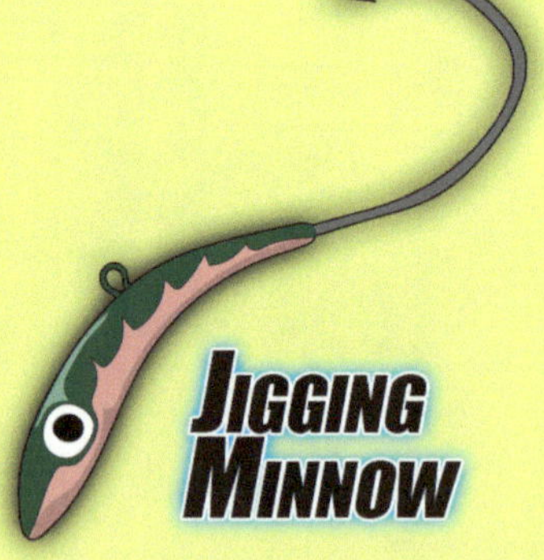

Bass Jig

Walking Surface Bait
Leech
Worm
Wire Leader
Swivel
Minnow
Minnow Trap
Spinning Reel
Spincast Reel

Spinning Rod
Spincast Rod

www.ingramcontent.com/pod-product-compliance
Lightning Source LLC
Chambersburg PA
CBHW042118110726
48006CB00002B/680